THE MUNCHY CRUNCHY BUGBOOK

Ray Nelson, Douglas Kelly, Ben Adams, and Julie Mohr

EDUCATION
FLYING RHINOCEROS
®

Dedicated To ...

The memory of Howard Raymond Adams
-Ben Adams

My two favorite parents, Jerry and Trisha Mohr
-Julie Mohr

Al Gottesman and Bob Savage
-Ray Nelson

My crazy Aunt Betteflo
-Douglas Kelly

ORKIN ®

Orkin Pest Control is committed to promoting education that provides a better understanding of the role that insects play in our natural environment. Although sometimes our homes need protection from those that "bug" us, insects play a critical role in our ecosystem. Like the O. Orkin Insect Zoo at the National Museum of Natural History at the Smithsonian Institution, which we sponsor, we hope that this book fascinates, educates and entertains. We are pleased to be a part of the sponsorship of The Munchy Crunchy Bug Book.

About Flying Rhinoceros books and curriculum materials

Flying Rhinoceros books are dedicated to the education and entertainment of elementary school students. Flying Rhinoceros also offers cross-curricular lesson plans and games to accompany all of its books. For more information, please contact Flying Rhinoceros at 1-800-537-4466.

Library of Congress Catalog Card Number: 97-060729
ISBN: 1-883772-08-7

Other books from Flying Rhinoceros:

The Seven Seas of Billy's Bathtub (Ocean and sea life)
Connie & Bonnie's Birthday Blastoff (Outer space)
Greetings from America (U.S. geography)
Shrews Can't Hoop!? (Self-esteem)
A Dinosaur Ate My Homework (Dinosaurs)
Wooden Teeth & Jelly Beans (U.S. presidents)
The Internal Adventures of Marcus Snarkis (Human Body)

visit us online:
www.flyingrhino.com

or call 1-800-537-4466

Introduction by Sally Love

For Fred Smertz, insects are delectable. For most people though, insects, or "bugs," are things that go bump in the night. And pester us during the day.

Why shouldn't we feel this way? Insects— crawling, flying, digging, and swimming all around—are so different from us they seem like science fiction aliens. Some of these tiny bugs even have the nerve to bite or sting. Ever wonder how big we look to them?

When I was younger, I used to sit and listen to the insect sounds that filled the air. I tried to understand their bizarre buzzes and chirps, but their language was too foreign. So I settled for imagining that I was an insect.

I could fly so fast, change my body shape as I grew up, eat all kinds of strange and disgusting foods, and float on a breeze for miles. It was fun!

I never forgot my early explorations and found that the more I learned about insects, the weirder they really were. I was hooked for life. Insects are fun to study and you don't have to travel to a remote rain forest to observe some of the cool things they do. Just turn over a rock, look under a leaf, watch them visit and pollinate a flower. You'll find they'll give you insights into the world around you—a planet that is vitally dependent on these small creatures.

So take a lesson from Fred—when you're hungry for some meat, bugs are more fun to watch than they are to eat!

Sally Love is an entomologist at the National Museum of Natural History Smithsonian Institution where she works studying insects of every shape, color and size imaginable.

WARNING!
Remember kids... Fred is not a normal child. You should never, ever eat a strange bug. Some insects are poisonous if eaten.

"TICK"
"TOCK"

"TICK"
"TOCK"

Upon a morning wet and dreary,
Fred Smertz slouches weak and weary.
"Why does the loyal classroom clock
so slowly tick...then slowly tock?
First tick, then tock. The classroom clock
reminds me of my trouble.
I've had to wait for far too long—
I swear I'm seein' double."

Behind his dark and musty desk,
the tired, worn-out boy
awaits, so very patiently,
the thing that brings him joy.

"**T**o stretch my legs and breathe fresh air,
remove my bottom from this chair —
that's what I need to make things swell.
I need to hear the recess bell!!!
Recess, ohhh, sweet recess —
the golden time approaches.
It sets me free to run and crawl
with spiders, ants, and roaches."

RRRIINNNGGGG

No other sound was ever so sweet.
Fred jumped in the air and flew from his seat,
down the main hall, and out the front door.
Fred was prepared for what was in store.
He shot 'cross the playground and headed due west
to his own secret place, the one he knows best.

CHOMP
CHOMP
CHOMP

The swamp, ahhh, the swamp — what a magical place!
It brings a big smile to little Fred's face.
"I'm here!" hollered Fred. "It's time to begin."
He licked his thin lips and wiped his big chin.
"Come out, come out, wherever you are.
It's time to be caught in an old jelly jar."

Just at that moment, out of the brush buzzed a plump Dragonfly in a bit of a rush.

WHAT IS AN INSECT?

Insects belong to a group of animals called Arthropoda (ar' thra po' duh).

Not every arthropod can be an insect!

Some arthropods just don't have what it takes to be an insect. Crustaceans (crabs, lobsters, and shimp), arachnids (spiders, scorpions, and mites), millipedes, and centipedes are arthropods, but they are not insects.

To be an insect you need all of the standard equipment!

standard equipment

1 Exoskeleton (pg 7)
3 Body parts (pg 8)
6 Legs (pg 8)
2 Antennae (pg 15)
2 Compound eyes (pg 16)

optional equipment

Wings, adults only (pg 11)
Simple eyes (pg 16)

Lots o' bugs

Insects, the biggest group of animals in the world, are found in almost every nook and cranny. Scientists have found about one million different insect species. There may actually be more than 30 million different insect species out there!

Dragonfly

Older than the dinosaurs!

Scientists think insects appeared about 400 million years ago. Some insects were a lot bigger in prehistoric times. A few Dragonflies had wingspans of more than two feet!

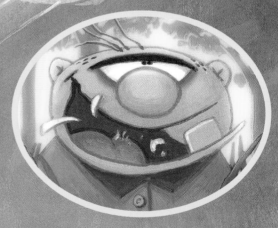

Before the dazed Dragonfly knew what to do,
Fred took a big bite and started to chew.

6

Fred started to sing his special bug song!

To the tune of "On Top of Old Smokey"

"**I** like eatin' buu-uugs. They taste good to me!
I can't stop with wuh-uuhn,
gotta have two or three."

"They buzz and they wiig-gle.....while I chomp 'em down! Then from deep in my tumm-my......you can still hear the sound. Bzz bzz bzz bzz bzzzz bzz.

standard equipment

1 Exoskeleton (ek' so skel' uh tun):
Insects' bodies are hard on the outside and soft on the inside. Their waterproof outer skeleton protects and supports their soft insides, like a suit of armor.

The exoskeleton is made of a material called chitin (kite' in).

People and many animals are soft on the outside and supported by a skeleton on the inside.

Room to move!

Exoskeletons are hard and can't stretch. So when an insect needs to grow, it wiggles out of, or sheds, its skeleton. This is called **molting**. The new exoskeleton starts out soft. Before it turns hard, the insect grows slightly larger. Young insects molt several times before reaching their adult size.

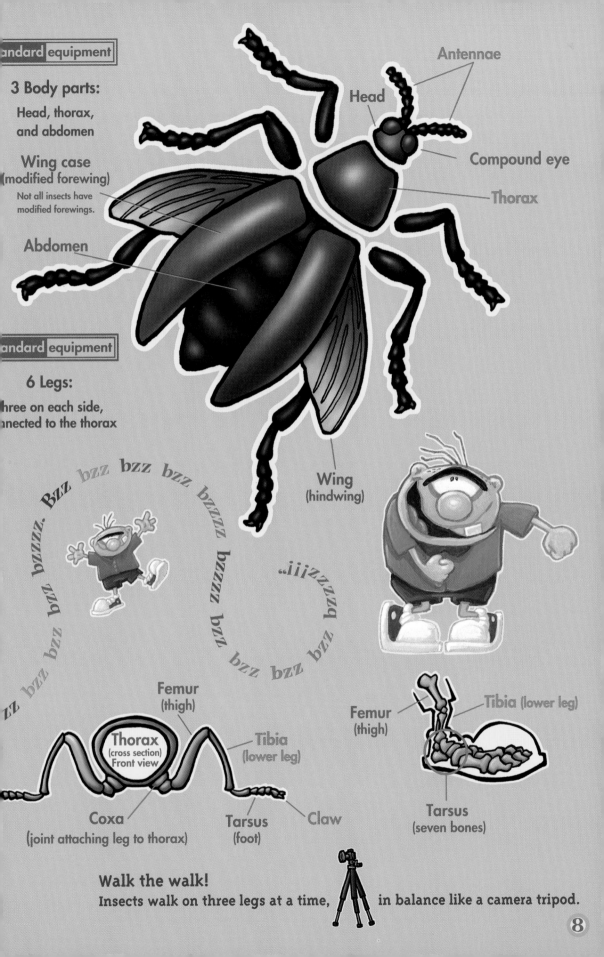

3 Body parts:
Head, thorax, and abdomen

Wing case (modified forewing)
Not all insects have modified forewings.

Abdomen

6 Legs:
three on each side, onnected to the thorax

Antennae

Head

Compound eye

Thorax

Wing (hindwing)

Bzz bzz bzz bzz bzz bzzzz bzzzz bzzzz bzz bzz bzz bzzzz bzz bzz bzz bzzzz ...iiizzz...

Femur (thigh)

Thorax (cross section) Front view

Tibia (lower leg)

Coxa (joint attaching leg to thorax)

Tarsus (foot)

Claw

Femur (thigh)

Tibia (lower leg)

Tarsus (seven bones)

Walk the walk!
Insects walk on three legs at a time, in balance like a camera tripod.

Now, you must realize that our little friend Fred,
as a very small child, fell on his head.
Some people say, since that terrible day,
that Fred tends to act in a rather odd way.
They say that his noggin isn't quite right,
just take a look at his strange appetite.

EATING AND BREATHING

Look out, midgut, here it comes!

Insects have a tube from
one end of their bodies
to the other.

Food goes down the throat, mixes
with saliva, and makes three stops
before food waste leaves the body.

1. **Foregut** (Food is ground up,
   and passed on to the midgut.)

2. **Stomach or midgut** (Food is broken
   down by digestive juices and absorbed.)

3. **Hindgut** (Excess water and salt is
   reabsorbed. Undigested food is carried away.)

Take a deep breath.

Insects don't have lungs.
They breath through openings
in their bodies called
spiracles (spear' uh kulz).

Food
goes in.

1
2
3

Food wa
comes c

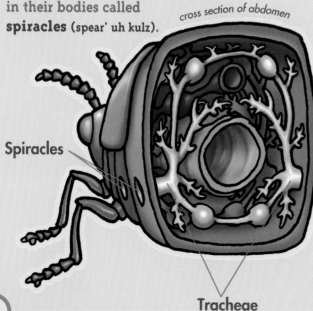

cross section of abdomen

Spiracles

Tracheae

Spiracles are on both sides of
an insect's abdomen and thorax.
The insect simply opens its spiracles
letting air into the **trachea** (tray' kee
Each trachea leads to a network
of tubes that branch out to
smaller tubes that supply
oxygen to the liquid interior,
organs, and muscles.

The bigger they are!

Big insects move more slowly than li
insects because it takes longer for
oxygen to reach all parts of a big
insect's body.

INSIDE A BUG

Blood bath

An insect's "heart" is one long tube. Muscles pump blood out an open end, and it proceeds to wash over the organs before returning to the heart.

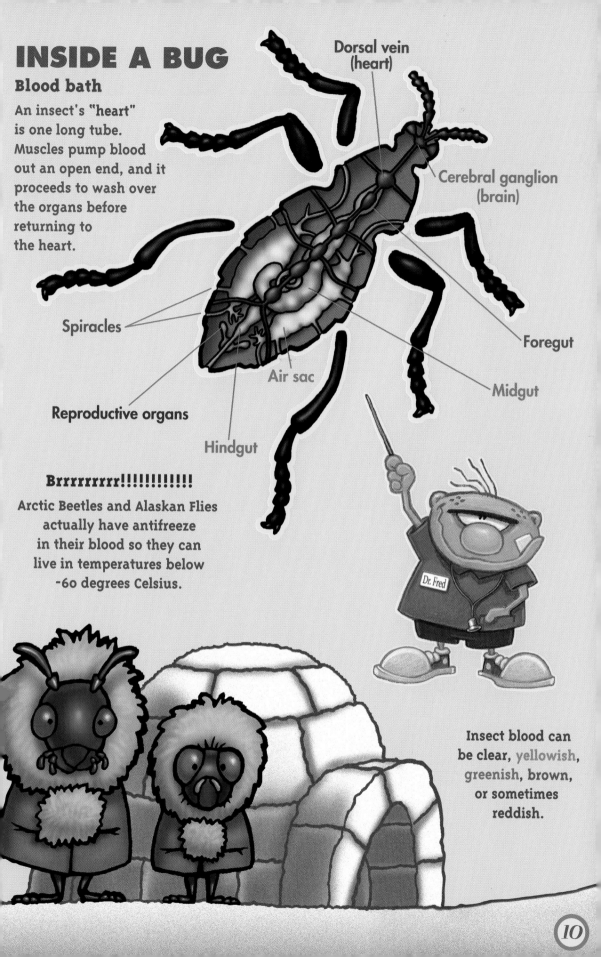

Dorsal vein (heart)

Cerebral ganglion (brain)

Spiracles

Foregut

Reproductive organs

Air sac

Midgut

Hindgut

Brrrrrrrrr!!!!!!!!!!!!!
Arctic Beetles and Alaskan Flies actually have antifreeze in their blood so they can live in temperatures below -60 degrees Celsius.

Dr. Fred

Insect blood can be clear, yellowish, greenish, brown, or sometimes reddish.

WINGS AND FLIGHT

Wing beats per second

Swallowtail (butterfly)..........5 beats
Honeybee.....................200 beats
Housefly.....................500 beats
Midge ("no-see-em").......1000 beats

Insects were the first creatures to fly.

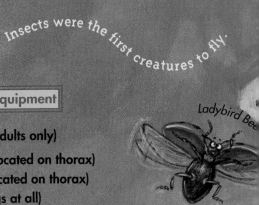

Ladybird Beetle

optional equipment

Wings (adults only)

2 pairs (located on thorax)
1 pair (located on thorax)
0 (no wings at all)

W hile most children love hot dogs and pies,

The wingspan of a female Atlas Moth can measure up to one foot.

Bee

Atlas Moth

F red craves the taste of black hairy flies.

Dragonfly can fly over
1 mph (miles per hour)
for short distances.

Red Skimmer

No muscles needed

Wings do not have muscles in them.
They are moved by big muscles that squeeze
within the thorax, thereby changing
the shape of the thorax.

Fight and flight

Insects use wings to get around, to get away from
danger, to attract a mate, and to defend or,
sometimes, to disguise themselves.

Grasshopper

Cockchafer
Beetle

Fly

Most wings are as thin as wax paper.

Periodical Cicada

He'll munch on a grub or a big juicy tick—
things that would make most kids queasy and sick.

12

Fred had just settled behind some big trees,
when he spotted a bug that was catching some Z's.
It was a wonderful specimen, juicy and plump –
a red and gold beetle with an oversized rump.

MOUTH PARTS

A hunting we will go...

Insects find food with their long antennae. Their palpi pull the food closer to their mouth parts.

Labrum (upper lip)

Damselfly

The Damselfly has a strong set of jaws, which enable it to tear its prey apart.

Great Green Bush-Cricket

Butterfly head

2 Mandibles (upper jaws)

Palpi

Bulldog Ant

Some insects, such as the Bulldog Ant, have long sharp jaws which can cause a painful bite.

Butterflies have a long tongue, called a proboscis (pruh boss' us), for sucking nectar from flowers.

House fly

Some mouthparts pierce ke needles, and suck plant uices or blood as through a drinking straw.

Male Stag Beetles joust other males with powerful jaws. They can actually chew through metals such as zinc and lead.

Flies lap up their food with a spongelike mouthpart.

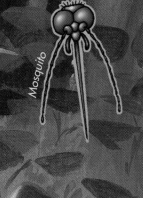

Mosquito

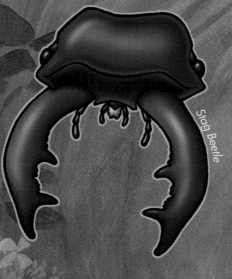

Stag Beetle

Fred

Fred Smertz has a tooth that is designed to rip and crush the legs, wings, and bodies of helpless insects.

> **F**red made his move – it was perfectly planned.
> He scooped the bug up in the palm of his hand.

SENSES

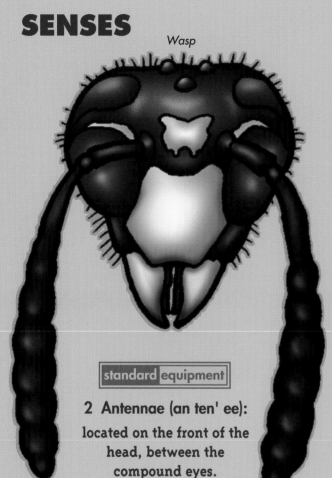

Wasp

Insects don't have noses, but sensory receptors on their antennae "smell" chemicals. This helps insects find food.

Insects don't have ears, but their antennae pick up vibrations from sound waves traveling through the air.

standard equipment

2 Antennae (an ten' ee): located on the front of the head, between the compound eyes.

Crickets have "ears" on their front le⟨ just below their kne⟨ This drumlike membrane is v⟨ sensitive to sound vibrations in the

Smelly feet

Butterflies taste with their feet. They land on a flower and walk around until they step in a pool of nectar, then they use their proboscises to suck it up.

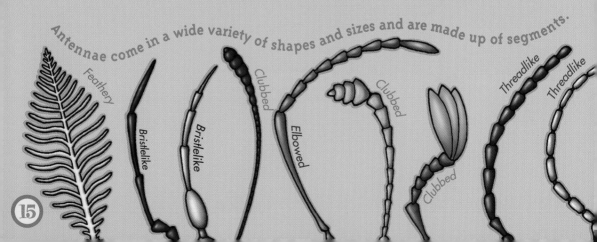

Antennae come in a wide variety of shapes and sizes and are made up of segments.

Feathery

Bristlelike

Bristlelike

Clubbed

Elbowed

Clubbed

Clubbed

Threadlike

Threadlike

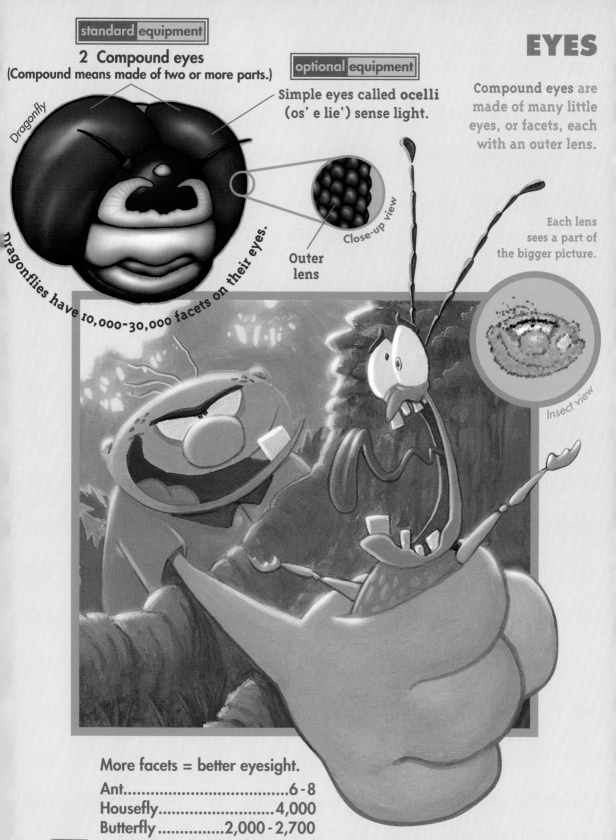

2 Compound eyes
(Compound means made of two or more parts.)

Dragonfly

Dragonflies have 10,000-30,000 facets on their eyes.

**Simple eyes called ocelli
(os' e lie') sense light.**

Close-up view

**Outer
lens**

Compound eyes are
made of many little
eyes, or facets, each
with an outer lens.

Each lens
sees a part of
the bigger picture.

Insect view

More facets = better eyesight.
Ant.....................................6-8
Housefly.........................4,000
Butterfly..............2,000-2,700

The bug was surprised by this sudden attack.
He was about to become a little bug snack.

GROWING UP

Insects have a different way of growing up called metamorphosis (met' a more' fuh sis). Metamorphosis means a change in form and in appearance. Most insects grow up in one of two ways: incomplete metamorphosis or complete metamorphosis.

Chinch B

1. Incomplete metamorphosis:

When an egg hatches into a new insect that looks like a small adult, it is called a nymph. As nymphs grow into adults they must **molt** several times.

He had to think fast to avoid his demise,
so he cleared his bug throat and blinked his bug eyes.
"I taste like old toe jam and smell like your feet.
You'd be sadly mistaken if you think I'm a treat!
So listen, my boy, to the secrets I tell
of other bug treats that taste really swell."

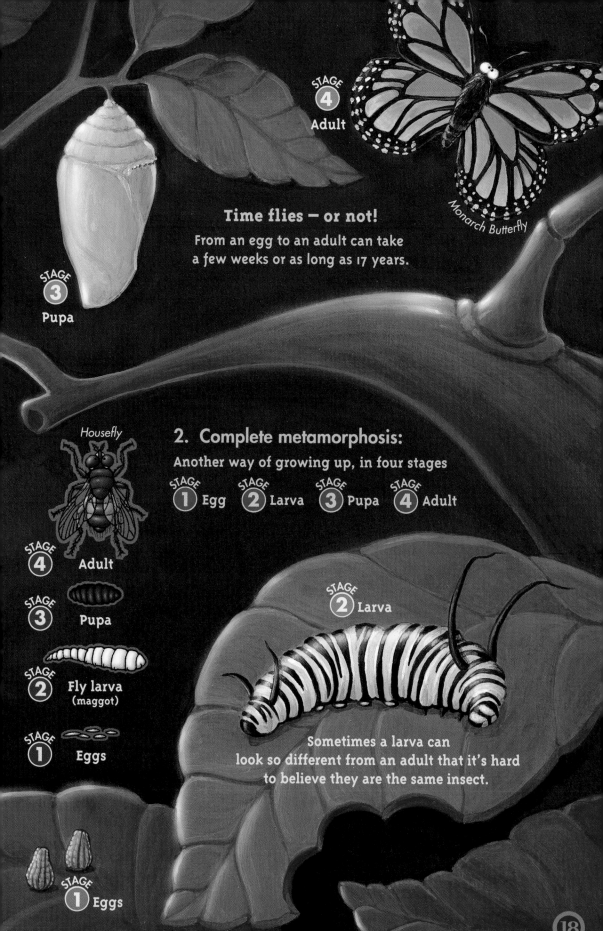

STAGE 4 Adult

Monarch Butterfly

STAGE 3 Pupa

Time flies – or not!

From an egg to an adult can take a few weeks or as long as 17 years.

Housefly

2. Complete metamorphosis:

Another way of growing up, in four stages

STAGE 1 Egg   **STAGE 2 Larva**   **STAGE 3 Pupa**   **STAGE 4 Adult**

STAGE 4 Adult

STAGE 3 Pupa

STAGE 2 Fly larva (maggot)

STAGE 1 Eggs

STAGE 2 Larva

Sometimes a larva can look so different from an adult that it's hard to believe they are the same insect.

STAGE 1 Eggs

Camouflage and Defenses

Insects have different ways of protecting themselves. Some imitate leaves, flowers, and even other insects. Others have developed ways to physically defend themselves against enemies.

Sticking Out
Long, slender Walking sticks hide among twigs and branches in perfect camouflage.

Giant walkingstick

The little bug's offer caught Fred by surprise. But what if this bug was telling bug lies?

Beware, crunchy one, if your offer goes south, you'll be squished like a bug and popped in my mouth!!

Shield stinckbugs

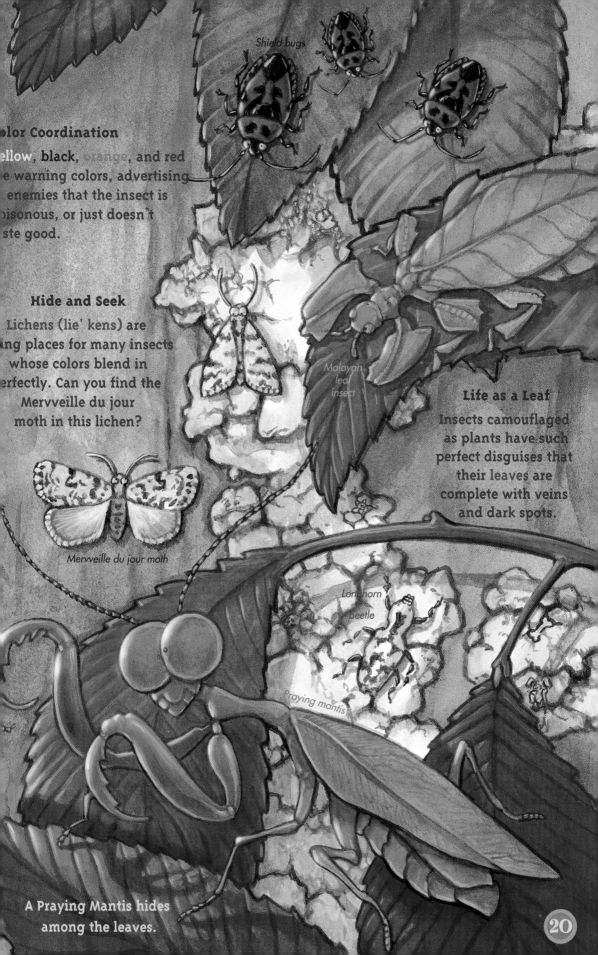

Shield bugs

ellow, black, orange, and red
e warning colors, advertising
enemies that the insect is
oisonous, or just doesn't
ste good.

Hide and Seek

Lichens (lie' kens) are
ing places for many insects
whose colors blend in
erfectly. Can you find the
Mervveille du jour
moth in this lichen?

Malayan
leaf
insect

Life as a Leaf

Insects camouflaged
as plants have such
perfect disguises that
their leaves are
complete with veins
and dark spots.

Mervveille du jour moth

Long-horn
beetle

Praying mantis

A Praying Mantis hides
among the leaves.

20

"**L**ook! Over there, up high in the sky!
It's a quick tasty snack, a big butterfly.
They're easy to catch as they wiggle and float,
and I guarantee pleasure as they slide down your throat!

BUTTERFLIES AND MOTHS

Moths and butterflies go throug
complete metamorphosis (pg 18

Female moths carry a perfume with them that they release when they are ready to attract a mate.

STAGE 1
Eggs

Moths lay large numbers of eggs.
Butterflies lay one or just a few eggs.

Tomato
Hornworm

STAGE 2

Woolly
Caterp

Larva

Both moth and butterfly larva
are caterpillars. They have chew
mouthparts for eating plants. Th
main purpose is to eat and
to go to stage 3.

chrysalis

STAGE 3
Pupa

cocoon

A moth caterpillar spins a cocoon
but a butterfly caterpillar forms
a chrysalis (kris' a lis).

Question Mark
Butterfly

STAGE 4
Adult

Large California
Spanworm Moth

Very different from the caterpillar, a new
creature comes out of resting. The adult mc
or butterfly has two pairs of wings and a suck
mouthpart. Their main focus is to find a ma

Mimi

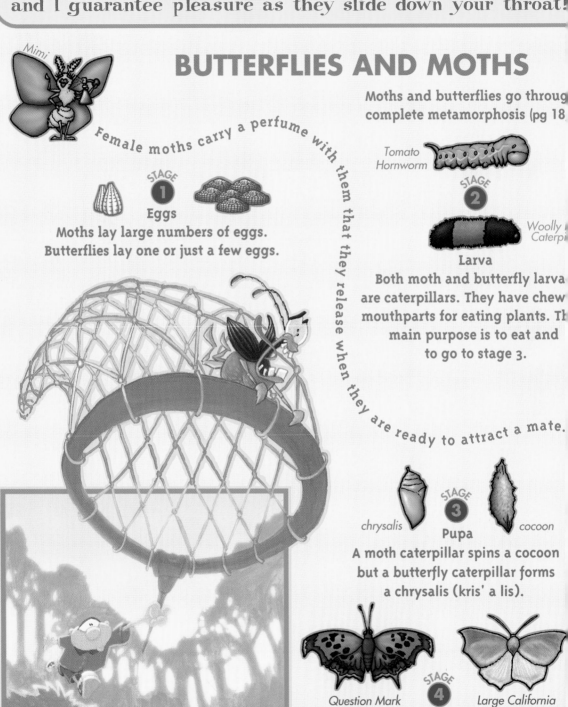

21

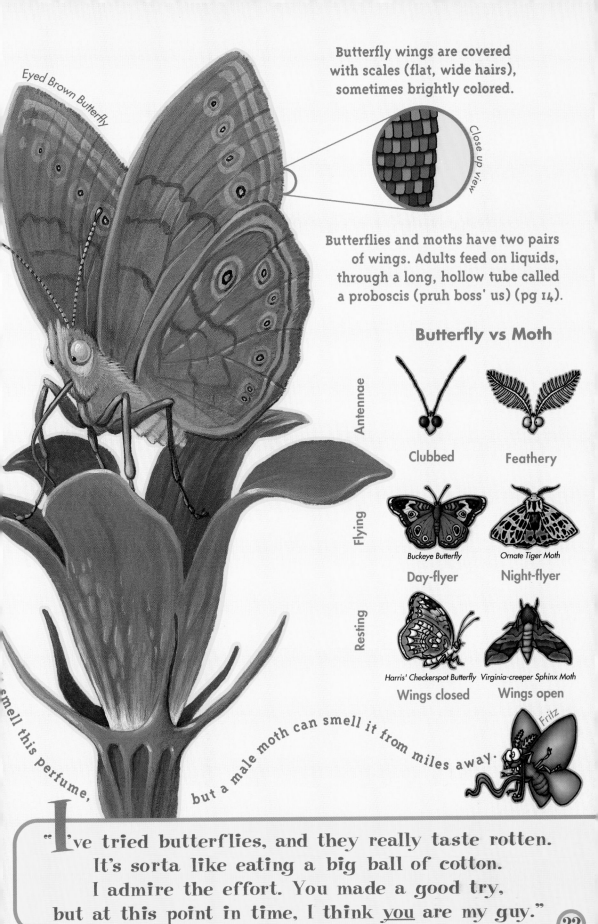

Eyed Brown Butterfly

Butterfly wings are covered with scales (flat, wide hairs), sometimes brightly colored.

Close up view

Butterflies and moths have two pairs of wings. Adults feed on liquids, through a long, hollow tube called a proboscis (pruh boss' us) (pg 14).

Butterfly vs Moth

Antennae

Clubbed

Feathery

Flying

Buckeye Butterfly

Ornate Tiger Moth

Day-flyer

Night-flyer

Resting

Harris' Checkerspot Butterfly

Virginia-creeper Sphinx Moth

Wings closed

Wings open

smell this perfume, but a male moth can smell it from miles away.

Fritz

"I've tried butterflies, and they really taste rotten.
It's sorta like eating a big ball of cotton.
I admire the effort. You made a good try,
but at this point in time, I think you are my guy."

22

Potters Wasp

Leafcutter Ants strip leaves from trees to grow fungus in underground gardens.

Guard dog ants!

Some members of the Leafcutter Ant colony sit on top of leaf pieces as they are being carried back to the nest. These ants help keep wasps from laying eggs on the worker ants' heads.

"May I offer to you the scrumptious red ant,
a delicacy found under any green plant?"
"You've got to be kidding. It's time to get real.
You'd need millions of ants for a decent-sized meal."
Fred gave a sigh and shook his round head,
"I think that it's best if I eat you instead."

But who cleans the little barn?

An ant colony has a strict social order. Each ant has a specific job that helps keep the colony up and running.

Queen
(fertile female)

Soldier
(sterile female)

Worker
(sterile female)

Male

ANT FARM

ANTS

A fungus among-us

Leafcutter Ants cut leaves from plants and chew them up to grow fungus in underground gardens. Other than plant sap, this fungus is their main food source.

One big happy family

Ants are social insects, most living in large groups called colonies. A colony can be made up of more than 20 million ants!

Living pantry

To prepare for the dry season in the deserts some Honeypot Ants turn into living storage tanks, holding food for the colony. They are fed extra nectar and honeydew, and can grow to the size of grapes.

BOOOOOM! Sometimes a Honeypot Ant falls from the ceiling and splits open.

Ant larvae are taken care of by their older sisters, the workers, who feed and protect them until they become adults.

Joe

Honeypot Ants

Bumble bee

The birds and the bees

When a bee lands on to a flower, pollen sticks to tiny hairs on its body. The bee pushes the pollen into special baskets on its back legs. When the bee moves onto another flower, some of the pollen falls or brushes off, thereby pollinating the second plant.

When a Honey Bee finds a food source, it returns to the hive and tells the others

"Bees!" yelled the beetle.
"What about bees?
They live all around
in the bushes and trees."
"I've tried eating bees,
but it wasn't too pleasant.
I popped one in my mouth
and got quite a present."

Bee positive

Honey Bee

Honeybees make and store
honey for winter food.

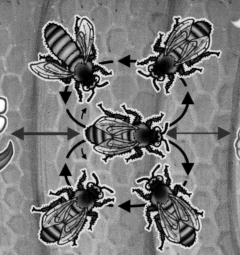

how to get there by doing a dance in a figure eight.

Honeybees use the sun to orient
themselves to food sources and back
to the hive. They pass that
information on to their sisters
using the "waggle dance."

There are 5-10 honey combs in an average hive.

The queen lays her eggs.

Busy as a bee

During late winter and
early spring, a queen bee
will lay as many as 2,000
eggs per day to rebuild
the population.

You're outta here!

Worker bees (females)
gather food, feed the young,
and maintain the hive. Drones
(male bees) can't feed themselves. Their only
job is to mate with the queen. They're kept as
long as there's enough food. Eventually
they're kicked out of the hive.

26

Damselfly

"Wait just a second! Don't give up yet. How 'bout a meal that's juicy and wet?"

Adult damselfly
STAGE 3

Dragonfly

Lunch on the fly

Dragonflies and Damselflies can spot a small insect 60 feet away, and grab it right out of the air while flying!

New adult breaks free of nymph exoskeleton
STAGE 2

Brown Stream Mayfly

Damselfly and dragonfly nymphs have gills to breathe underwater.

STAGE 1
Damselfly nymph

Take a deep breath

In order to breathe underwater, some insects carry an air bubble with them.

Diving Beetle

27

WATERBUGS

Madame Dracula
Only female mosquitoes bite— a
blood meal helps fertilize her eggs.

Anopheline Mosquito

Dragonfly

Quit bugging me!

A species of tropical
mosquito carries the parasite
that causes malaria. Malaria
kills one million people
every year.

Slippery when wet

Water Striders can "walk on water."
They are very light and their feet are coated
with a waxy substance that keeps the surface
tension of the water from breaking.

Bob

Water Striders

Close-up view

Water Boatman

Mosquito larvae

Fred stared at the beetle, feeling provoked.
"Pond skaters are thin, and my socks would get soaked!
I'm getting real hungry and I think you're a faker.
It's time, my small friend, to meet your Bug Maker."

"Spiders have a taste that will make your pulse quicken.
It's a flavor, I'm told, that resembles fried chicken!"
"Spiders!" Fred shouted. "That simply won't do.
They bite really hard–I know this is true."

SPIDERS

Spiders have an exoskeleton and molt like insects but are not true insects, they are Arachnids (a rack' nidz). Other arachnids include scorpions, mites, and ticks.

Silky trap!

Orb Weaver Spiders spin sticky silk webs to catch insects and make them a meal.

Spiny
Orb Weaver

Orb Weaver Spider

paralyzed food
wrapped up
for later

Grass Spider

Brown Daddy Longlegs

Raft Spider

Daddy Longlegs
are Arachnids, but they aren't spiders. They can't spin silk, and will eat plants and living or dead insects.

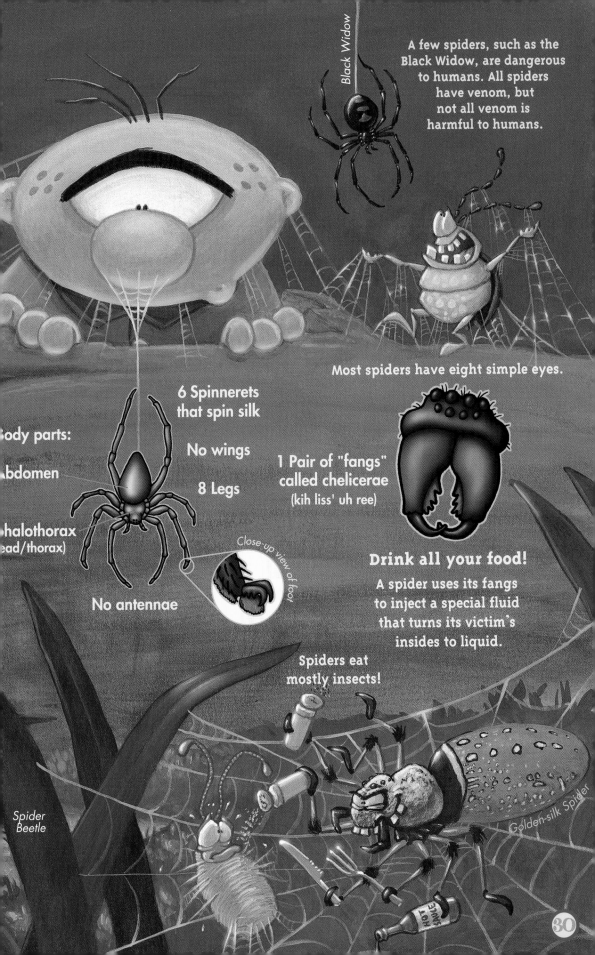

A few spiders, such as the Black Widow, are dangerous to humans. All spiders have venom, but not all venom is harmful to humans.

Most spiders have eight simple eyes.

6 Spinnerets that spin silk

No wings

8 Legs

Body parts:

Abdomen

Cephalothorax
(head/thorax)

No antennae

Close-up view of foot

1 Pair of "fangs" called chelicerae (kih liss' uh ree)

Drink all your food!

A spider uses its fangs to inject a special fluid that turns its victim's insides to liquid.

Spiders eat mostly insects!

Spider Beetle

Golden-silk Spider

"**L**ook all around and I think that you'll see
not all of my cousins taste yucky like me.
Big honkin' beetles live above and beneath.
The only drawback is they stick in your teeth."

There are more than 300,000 different kinds
of beetles (1/3 of all known insects).

Colorado
Potato Beetle

Chafer
Beetle

Blackoak
Acorn Weevil

Elegant
Checkered Beetle

Metallic
Beetle

BIG, BIG, BIG small, small, small

Beetles have some of the largest and smallest
members of all known insect groups.
The largest beetle is the Hercules Beetle,
which can be almost 6 1/2 inches long.
The Feather-winged Beetle is so small
it can sit on the head of a pin.

u're gonna do what with that?

.ating pair of Dung Beetles will find a piece of animal dung (poop), roll it into a ball,
roll it back to their burrow. The female will lay an egg in the center. This will be the
ching grub's first few meals.

Scarab Beetle symbolizes the
ncient Egyptian sun god Ra.

Dung
Beetle

Ironclad Beetle

Black Pine Sawyer
Beetle

Leaf Beetle

ig fat cow

he Goliath Beetle is the heaviest
sect in the world. It can weigh
.4 ounces— almost as much
s a quarter-pound
heeseburger.

One tough beetle

Beetles have the toughest exoskeletons of all insects.
Some are so strong that it takes a hammer to stick
pins through the preserved specimens for collecting.

Jewel Beetle

Goliath Beetle

Giraffe
Beetle

Firefly

Flashdance

Fireflies are beetles, not flies.
A firefly flashes at night to attract a mate.
The "light" is generated by a chemical in the firefly's body.

"**J**ust over there – beyond the great bog,
under that tree, in an old rotten log –
is a snack that, believe me, tastes rather good.
Its flavor reminds some of old rotting wood."

**Termite colonies
can house up to five
million termites.**

That's heavy, man

The total weight of all the
termites on Earth is almost
twice the total weight of
all the people.

The queen shown below is an African Termite queen.

macrotermes

Worker

Soldier

**When does she
have time for tea?**

A termite queen can live for 15 years,
and can lay an egg every three
seconds for her entire life.

TERMITES

These guys need an elevator

Some termites in Africa build mud
nests that tower 30 feet tall!
(That would be like people building
a skyscraper 1,300 stories high!)
Below the surface are caverns
as deep as 32 feet!

Dinner guests

Termites eat wood, but they can't digest it. Microscopic organisms
called protozoa (pro¯ta zo⁺ a) live in the termites' guts, and
digest the wood for them. Without these protozoa,
termites would starve to death.

Soldier

Worker

Take one more step
and I'll explode on you!

Some termite soldiers defend their nest by exploding
and spraying their enemy with sticky guts.
Other termite soldiers spray poison
from spouts on their heads.

Male

One big happy family

Termites have families similar
to ants and bees. The termite
family is made up of a queen,
a king, workers, and soldiers.

Young nymph

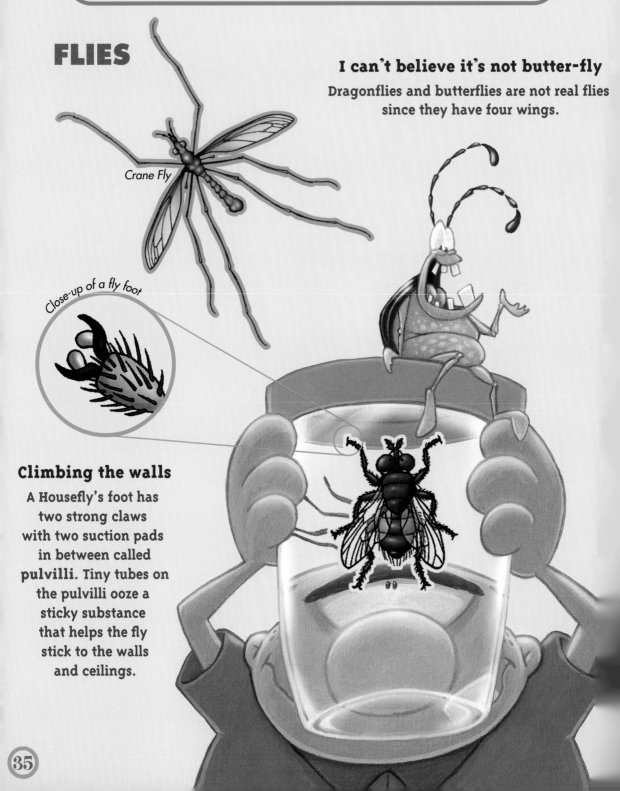

"**A**nother suggestion resides in your hair -
a real tasty tidbit you need not prepare.
Reach right on up and give it a try.
The snack that you need is a nice juicy fly!"

FLIES

Crane Fly

I can't believe it's not butter-fly

Dragonflies and butterflies are not real flies
since they have four wings.

Close-up of a fly foot

Climbing the walls

A Housefly's foot has
two strong claws
with two suction pads
in between called
pulvilli. Tiny tubes on
the pulvilli ooze a
sticky substance
that helps the fly
stick to the walls
and ceilings.

Stunt flyer

Flies can fly forward or backward or hover in one spot.

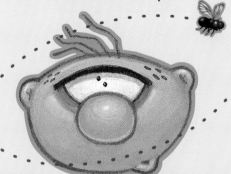

Who wants a drumstick?

True flies have only one pair of wings. They also have a pair of little bumps on their back that look like drumsticks, called **halters**. Halters help the fly keep its balance.

House Fly

It's a fly-eat-frog world out there!

Horsefly larvae hide in the mud waiting for young Spade-foot Toads to come out of the water. The larva hooks onto the toad, injects it with venom, and sucks the toad dry, leaving a crisp, shriveled corpse.

Horse Fly

A milkshake for every meal!

A fly can only eat liquid food. If its food is solid, it "throws up" a substance that dissolves the food into a liquid.

Bee impostors

Some flies actually look like bees. This helps fool predators into thinking they'll get stung.

Hover Fly

Bee Fly

Wingin' it

Some grasshoppers have brightly colored hindwings that are hidden until they lift their forewings. The flash of color can confuse enemies.

Band-winged Grasshopper

Quit bugging me!

Locusts are grasshoppers that sometimes cause big problems. The largest recorded swarm of locusts was made up of 40 billion locusts — eight times the number of all human beings on Earth!

The leathery forewings of grasshoppers and crickets are called **tegmina** (teg' muh nuh). They are not used for flying, but protect the hindwings.

Field Cricket

Carolina Locust

Mormon Cricket

Listen, my friend. Do you hear what I hear?
The beautiful sound of chirping is near.
Crickets and hoppers taste great night or day,
and they work really well for a quick getaway.

HOPPERS & CRICKETS

Pump you up
The muscles in a locust's hind legs are one thousand times stronger than an equal amount of human muscle.

Painted Grasshopper

The grasshopper uses its leg and wing like a violin: the leg is the bow and the wing vein is the string. The cricket uses only its wings to "sing."

Mole Cricket

The male Mole Cricket lives in a burrow with two openings that help amplify his song. You could hear him 650 yards away.

38

The beetle rode fast and the beetle rode far,
but he was no match for Fred's jelly jar.
The beetle had come to the end of his rope—
he was just about ready to give up all hope.
"I really don't know what it is I should do,
so please listen, Fred, while I reason with you."

Up all night

Cockroaches are nocturnal. During the day their thin, flat bodies let them squeeze into small cracks to hide.

Help! I'm losing my mind!

A cockroach can live for up to nine days without its head.

There are 5,000 different types of cockroaches.

On your mark, get set...

A cockroach is the fastest thing on six legs, traveling up to five feet per second.

COCKROACHES

Oriental Cockroach

Please pass the lint...

Cockroaches can live almost anywhere and eat almost anything. Some can live for months eating nothing but dust.

American cockroach

Silverfish

Cockroach

Earwig

"Fred, you must learn how important bugs are.
We shouldn't be trapped in an old jelly jar.
We dispose of gross things other creatures ignore,
and we help make the fruit that you buy in the store."

"This is your chance, so reach out and grab it.
Once and for all stop your bug-eating habit!"
This beetle was amazing—he was really quite grand.
Fred held him up high in the palm of his hand.

He said with a giggle, "I really don't mind
being sidetracked by you. You're one of a kind!"

"This day, yes indeed, turned out to be fun.
In Fred Smertz's book, you're A-number-one."

Fred ran back to class with mud on his feet.
He crashed through the door and slouched in his seat.
"This has been a super-spectacular-wonderful day—
I expanded my brain and still got to play.
I learned what bugs eat, where they live, what they do,
and that beetles—yes, beetles—crunch when you chew."

Glossary

amber · fossilized tree resin that is considered a precious stone.

arthropods · a group of invertebrates, including insects, crustaceans, arachnids, millipedes, and centipedes.

chelicerae · a pair of fangs located in the front of a spider's mouth.

chitin · a substance related to sugar that makes up most of the exoskeleton of an insect.

complete metamorphosis · the change of larva to adult through a series of stages.

elytra · the hardened forewing covering of a beetle.

exoskeleton · the hard protective structure that all insects have on the outside of their bodies.

halteres · two knobby structures in place of the second pair of wings that help a fly keep its balance while flying.

incomplete metamorphosis · the change of a nymph to an adult, the most common type of metamorphosis.

larva/larvae · young insects that have not yet changed to adults and do not even resemble adults. This is a stage in complete metamorphosis.

mandibles · the jaws of an insect.

nocturnal · active at night.

nymph · a young insect that resembles an adult but is still going through incomplete metamorphosis.

ovipositor · the part of an insect that lays eggs.

parthenogenesis · producing young without fertilization.

pulvilli · the cushioned pads between an insect's toes.

pupa · the form a larva takes during complete metamorphosis to undergo the change from larva to adult; often enclosed in a cocoon.

queen substance · a chemical produced by the queen among social insects that makes workers unable to reproduce.

royal jelly · the food source created to produce young queens in social insect colonies.

setae · tiny, sensitive hairs that cover an insect's exoskeleton.

spiracles · breathing holes along the sides of an insect's exoskeleton.

spinneret · the body part on a spider (and some moth caterpillars) that spin silk.

taxonomic system · the scientific system that distinguishes different groups of plants and animals, including insects.

tracheae · the system of breathing tubes that are found throughout an insect's body.

vertical and horizontal muscles · the muscles that control the movement of an insect's wings.

Ray Nelson is scared of big hairy spiders. When he was a boy, he lived on a farm. A giant spider carried away his prize-winning cow. Today, Ray hangs several hundred no-pest strips around his house Portland, Oregon. His wife Theresa and daughter Alexandria actually like spiders and tease Ray all the ti about his fear. The Nelsons have a Great Dane named Molly who eats spiders for fun.

Douglas Kelly is about the size of a Praying Mantis. One time Doug actually got stuck in one of Ray's no-pest strips for six days. He lives with his cat, Toonces, in Eugene, Oregon. Doug spends most of spare time listening to jazz and chasing a little white ball all over golf courses in the Pacific Northwest.

Ben Adams eats worms. After he gets his fill of worms, he enjoys listening to heavy metal music and building monster model kits. Ben lives in an apartment overlooking Portland, Oregon. It has a beaut view and a garden full of all the worms he can eat.

Julie Mohr has a pet Walking Stick named Spot. She and Spot have been friends since Julie was a small girl growing up in Tillamook, Oregon. Spot actually saved Julie from a burning mine shaft during flood of '74. Julie and Spot currently live in Tualatin, Oregon.

A special thanks to Sally Love, J.R. Williams, Cindy Duft, Deborah Beilman, Mike and Holly McLane, Lynnea Eagle, Chris Nelson, Ranjy Thomas, Kyle Holveck, Ray Nelson, Sr., Doug Holladay, Frank Vizcar